Searchlight BOOKS™

How Does Energy Work?

Investigating Magnetism

Sally M. Walker

Lerner Publications Company
Minneapolis

Author's note: The experiments in this book use the metric measurement system, as that's the system most commonly used by scientists.

Lerner Publications Company
A division of Lerner Publishing Group, Inc.
241 First Avenue North
Minneapolis, MN 55401 U.S.A.

Website address: www.lernerbooks.com

Library of Congress Cataloging-in-Publication Data

Walker, Sally M.
Investigating magnetism / by Sally M. Walker.
p. cm. — (Searchlight books™—How does energy work?)
Includes index.
ISBN 978-0-7613-5775-9 (lib. bdg. : alk. paper)
1. Magnetism—Juvenile literature. 2. Magnetism—Experiments—Juvenile literature. 3. Magnets—Juvenile literature. I. Title.
QC753.7.W35 2012
538—dc22 2010039848

Manufactured in the United States of America
1 – DP – 7/15/11

Contents

Chapter 1

MAGNETS

Look around your home or classroom. Do you see any magnets? Many people use magnets to hold pictures on their refrigerators. These magnets are easy to see.

Some magnets are easy to see. Other magnets are hidden inside machines. What do the hidden magnets do?

Without magnets, earbuds wouldn't work.

There are also many magnets that you can't see. They are hidden inside earbuds, telephones, and computers. Why are magnets inside these items?

A magnet makes magnetic force. A force is a push or a pull. Magnetic force makes a magnet stick to a refrigerator. Forces from hidden magnets make many machines work.

Atoms

A magnet's force begins with tiny particles called atoms. Everything is made of atoms. Magnets, air, plants, rocks, and your body are made of atoms. Billions of atoms could fit on the dot of the letter *i*. The center of an atom is called the nucleus.

Everything around you is made of atoms. You are made of atoms too!

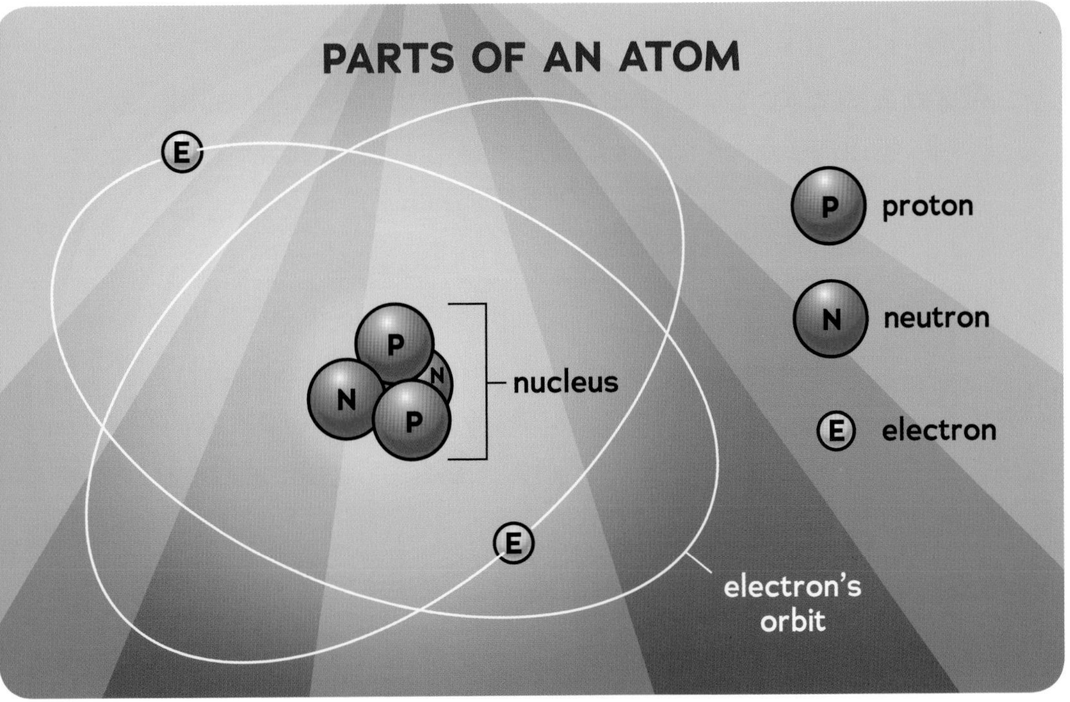

Atoms are made of even smaller particles. These particles are called protons, neutrons, and electrons. An atom's nucleus is made of protons and neutrons. Electrons orbit around an atom's nucleus. Orbiting is traveling in a circle. A little bit of a magnet's force is made by electrons orbiting inside it.

Move Like an Electron

Ask a friend to sit in the middle of the room. Walk in a circle around your friend. You are orbiting your friend. While an electron is orbiting, it also moves in a second way. Stop walking and stand in place. Spin your body around. An electron spins this way too. Most of a magnet's force comes from electrons spinning inside it.

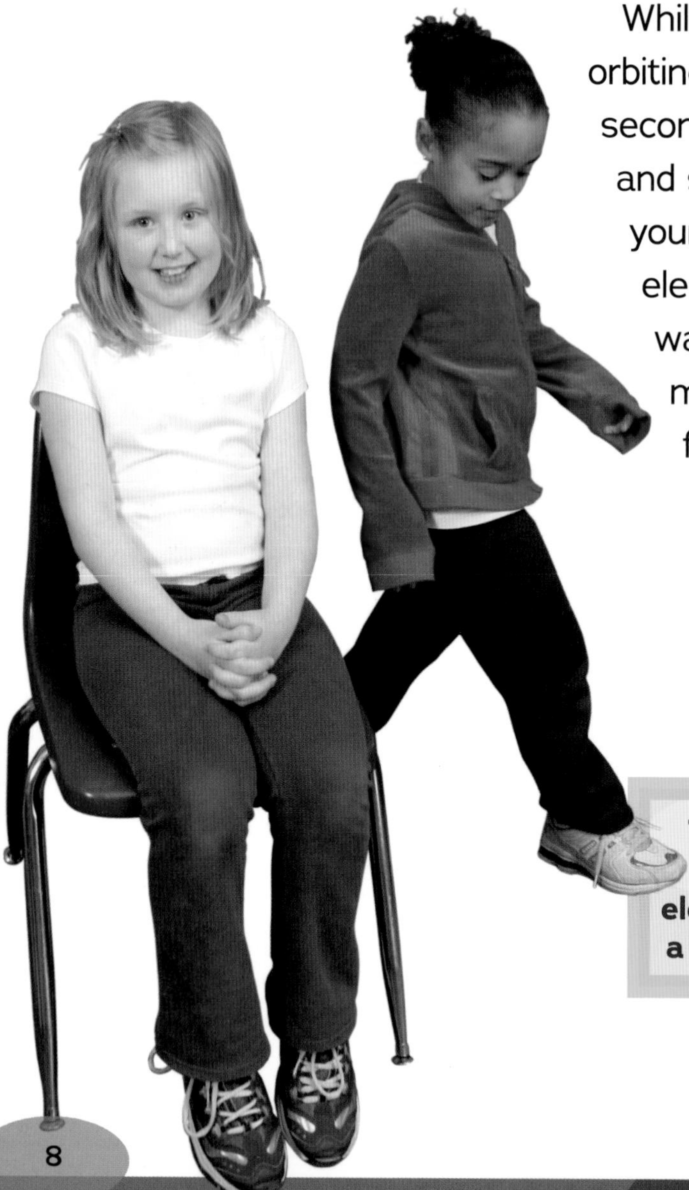

The girl who is walking is pretending to be an electron. She is moving in a circle around her friend.

Now the girl is spinning in place. An electron spins while it is moving in a circle around a nucleus.

An atom's electrons spin in different directions. Some electrons spin clockwise. The rest spin counterclockwise. Sometimes half of an atom's electrons spin clockwise and half spin counterclockwise. Then the atom has no magnetic force. But if more electrons spin one way than the other, the atom has magnetic force. Atoms that have magnetic force act like tiny magnets.

Chapter 2

MAGNETIC MATERIALS

Some magnets are stronger than others. Strong magnets have more magnetic force than weak magnets. Bar magnets, horseshoe magnets, and round magnets are strong. But rubbery refrigerator magnets are weak.

Strong magnets lift heavy pieces of metal in junkyards. Do all magnets keep their magnetic force forever?

Permanent Magnets and Temporary Magnets

Some magnets are permanent magnets. Permanent magnets keep their magnetic force forever. Other magnets are temporary magnets. Temporary magnets keep their magnetic force for a while. But then it goes away.

A kind of black rock called lodestone is a permanent magnet. Some metals can become permanent magnets too. Iron, nickel, steel, and cobalt are metals that can be made into permanent magnets. Materials that can be made into magnets are called magnetic materials.

Nickels are named after the metal called nickel. That's because these coins are made of copper that has some nickel mixed into it.

A Strong Attraction

A magnet attracts other magnetic materials. The magnet's force pulls on the magnetic material. The pulling force makes the magnetic material stick to the magnet. Magnets stick to any magnetic material.

The metal strip on this counter is made of magnetic material. The magnets stick to it.

Experiment Time!

Get a magnet and a paper clip. Can you pick up the paper clip with the magnet? Yes. The magnet attracts the paper clip. The paper clip is made of steel. Steel is a magnetic material.

Most materials are nonmagnetic. Magnets don't attract nonmagnetic materials. And nonmagnetic materials can't be made into magnets. The metals aluminum, copper, and silver are nonmagnetic. So are rubber, wood, and concrete.

Paper clips are made of steel. Magnets attract objects that are made of steel.

A magnet can't pick up a wooden pencil.

Use your magnet to find out if materials are magnetic. Does your magnet stick to the glass in a window? Can your magnet pick up a pencil? Test other materials. See if they are magnetic or not.

Chapter 3

HOW MAGNETS WORK

Every magnet has a magnetic field. The magnetic field is a space around the magnet. Inside this space, the magnet's force can attract an object. If magnetic material is outside the field, the magnet can't attract it. You can prove this.

Magnets attract steel objects like paper clips. Why isn't this magnet attracting the paper clips?

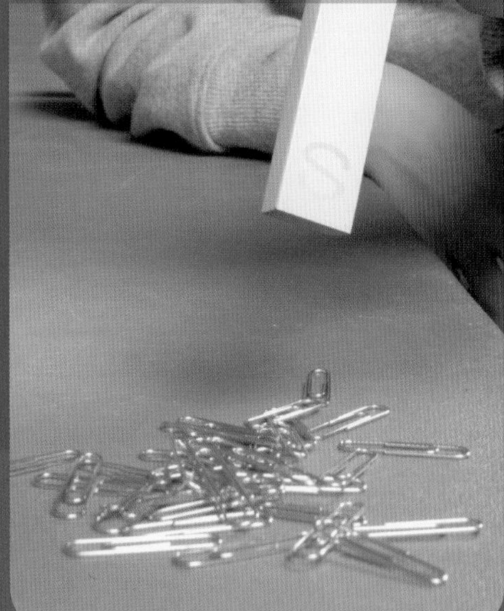

Trying It Out

You'll need a piece of thread, a metal paper clip, and a magnet. Tie one end of the thread to the paper clip. Put the paper clip on a table. Use your finger to hold the thread's loose end against the table. Put the magnet about 25 centimeters away from the paper clip. Move the magnet up and down. Is the paper clip attracted to the magnet? No. The paper clip just stays still. The paper clip is outside the magnetic field. The magnet can't attract the paper clip.

The paper clip is outside the magnet's magnetic field. So the magnet can't attract the paper clip.

Put the magnet about 1 centimeter from the paper clip. Lift the magnet up and down. What happens now? The paper clip moves. It is inside the magnetic field.

Magnetic force is strongest close to the magnet. Sometimes the force is strong enough to lift an object without touching it. Can your magnet lift the paper clip off the table without touching it?

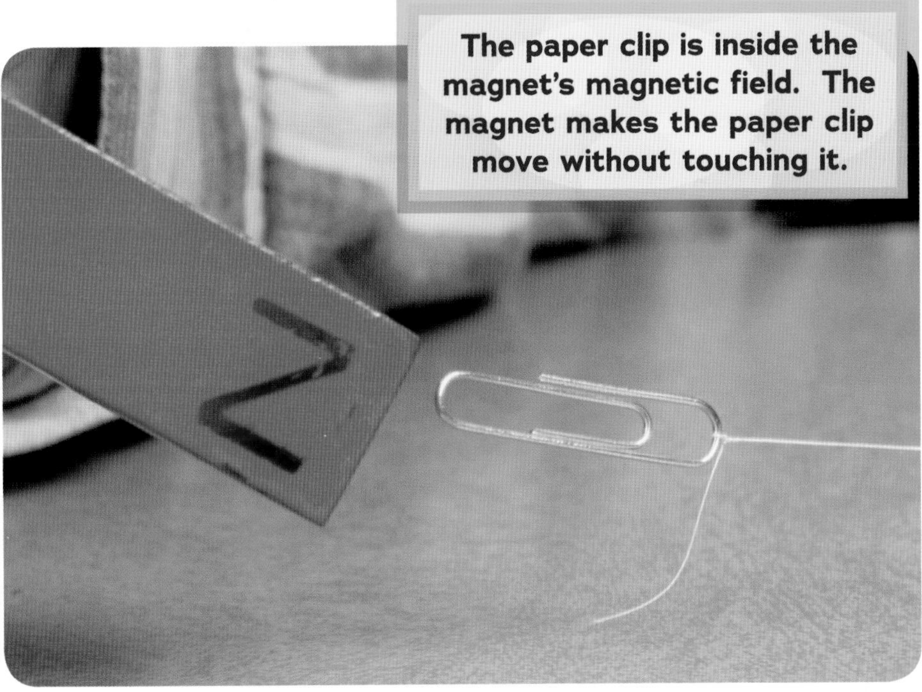

The paper clip is inside the magnet's magnetic field. The magnet makes the paper clip move without touching it.

Chapter 4

MAGNETIC POLES

Two parts of a magnet have the strongest pulling power. These parts are called poles. Every magnet has two poles. One is called the north pole. The other is called the south pole.

The two ends of a horseshoe magnet attract magnetic material. What are the two ends called?

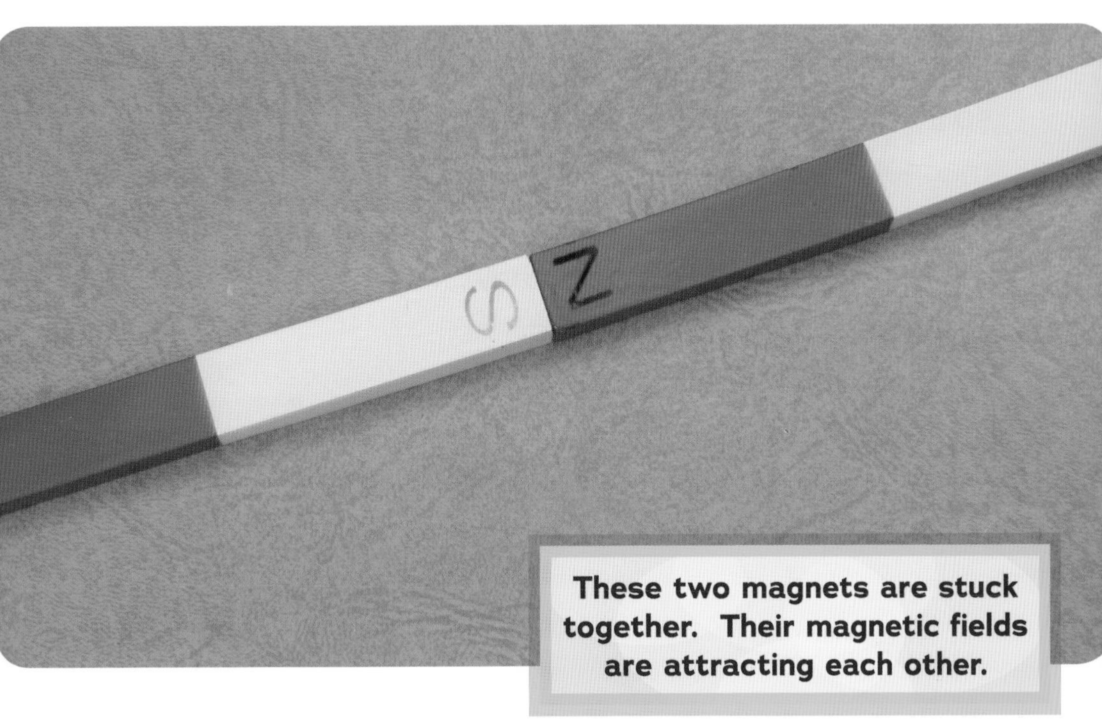

These two magnets are stuck together. Their magnetic fields are attracting each other.

The magnetic field of one magnet can affect the magnetic field of another magnet. The two magnetic fields push or pull at each other. The magnets try to line up so both magnetic fields point in the same direction.

Earth's Magnetic Field

Earth has a magnetic field. So Earth has a magnetic north pole. If you hang a magnet from a string, it turns so its magnetic field lines up with Earth's field. The magnet's north pole will always point toward Earth's magnetic north pole. The needle of a compass is a magnet. The needle's north pole turns until it points toward Earth's magnetic north pole.

EARTH'S MAGNETIC FIELD

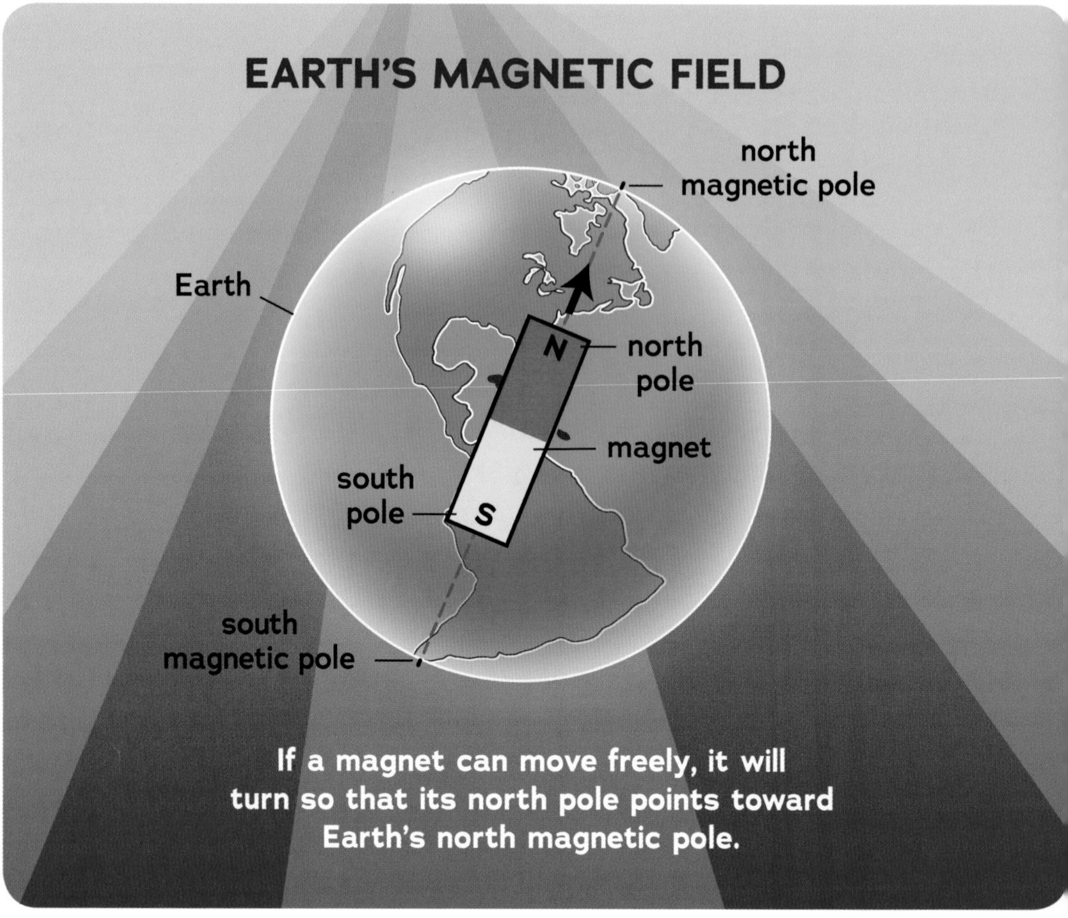

If a magnet can move freely, it will turn so that its north pole points toward Earth's north magnetic pole.

Experiment Time Again!

You can find a magnet's north pole. You will need a scissors, a thick foam plate, tape, two small bar magnets, a pen, a compass, and a large bowl of water.

Cut two strips of foam. Each strip should be longer and wider than the magnets. Tape one magnet to each foam strip. Draw an *X* on the foam next to one end of each magnet. The *X* will help you tell the ends apart.

If the foam is too thin, the magnet will not float. If your magnet doesn't float, cut extra strips of foam. Tape three or four strips together to make one thick strip of foam.

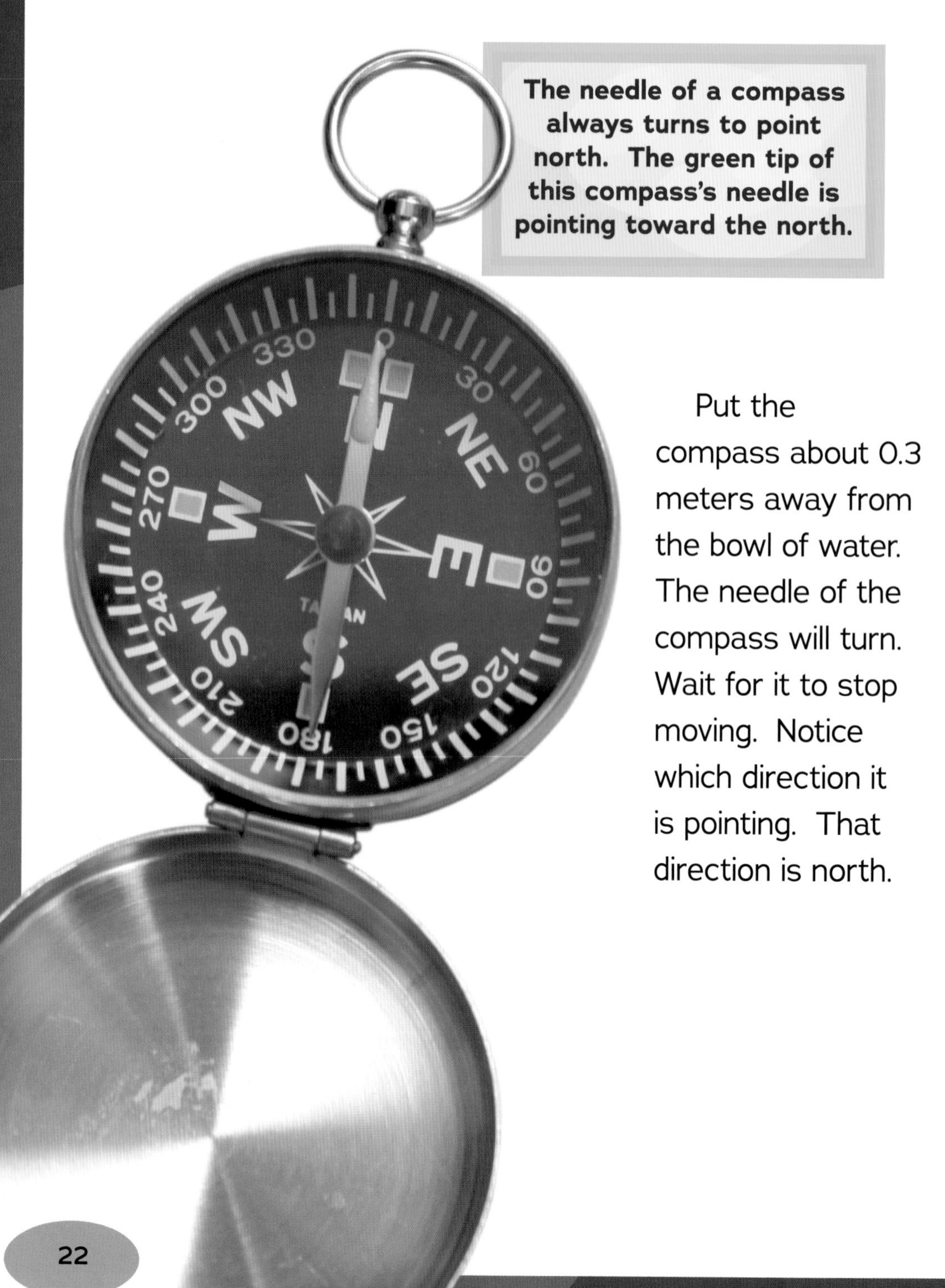

The needle of a compass always turns to point north. The green tip of this compass's needle is pointing toward the north.

Put the compass about 0.3 meters away from the bowl of water. The needle of the compass will turn. Wait for it to stop moving. Notice which direction it is pointing. That direction is north.

Float one of the magnets in the bowl of water. Watch as the magnet turns. One end always turns toward the north. That end is the magnet's north pole. The other end is the south pole. Turn the float around, and then let go. The magnet will turn back around to point north.

Put a tiny piece of tape on the magnet's north pole. Mark it with an *N*. Find the other magnet's north pole the same way.

The end of the magnet that points in the same direction as the compass's needle is the magnet's north pole.

Take the magnets off the foam floats. Hold each magnet by its south pole. Try to make the two north poles touch. What happens? The magnets push away from each other. Hold the two north poles. Try to touch the south poles together. The same thing happens. Why? Because poles that are alike repel each other. Repelling is pushing away.

Even if you push hard, you can't make two north poles touch.

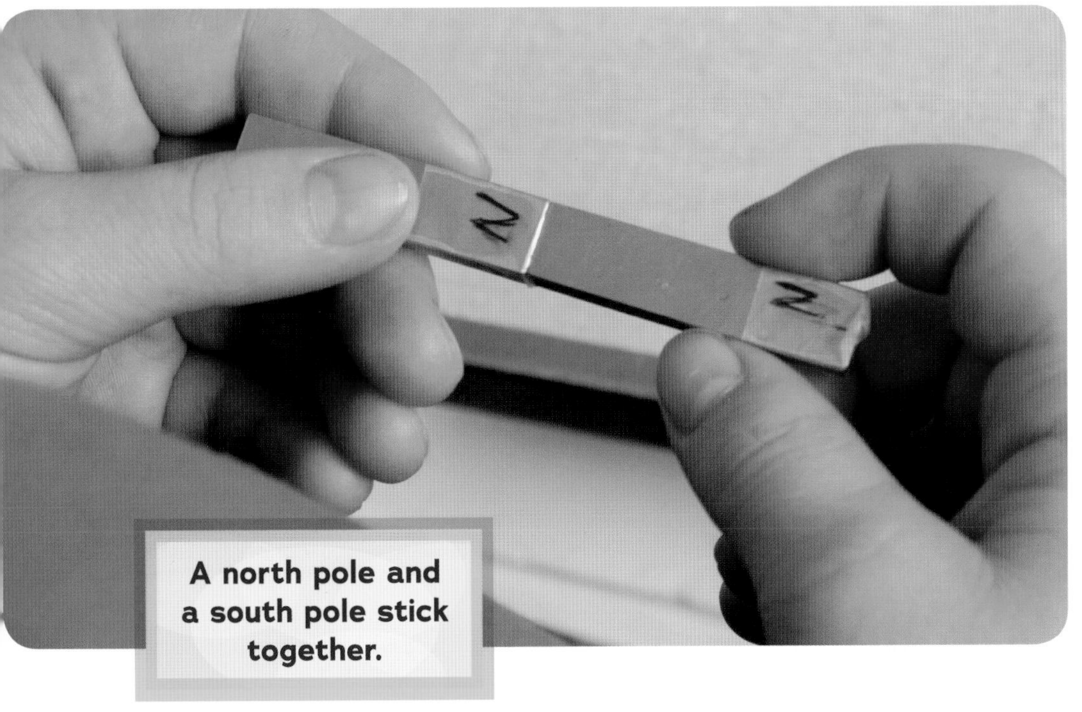

A north pole and a south pole stick together.

Hold one magnet by its north pole. Hold the other magnet by its south pole. Try to touch the magnets together. What happens? They stick together. Why? Because unlike poles attract each other. Unlike poles are poles that are different.

Put one magnet on a table. Can you push the magnet off the table without touching it? Push it with magnetic force. Remember that like poles repel each other. And unlike poles attract each other.

Use the north pole of one magnet to push against the north pole of the other magnet.

Magnetic force can work through nonmagnetic materials. Cover a paper clip with a piece of paper. Hold a magnet very close to the paper. Lift the magnet. What happens? The magnetic force passes through the paper. The magnet attracts the paper clip. The magnet lifts both the paper and the paper clip.

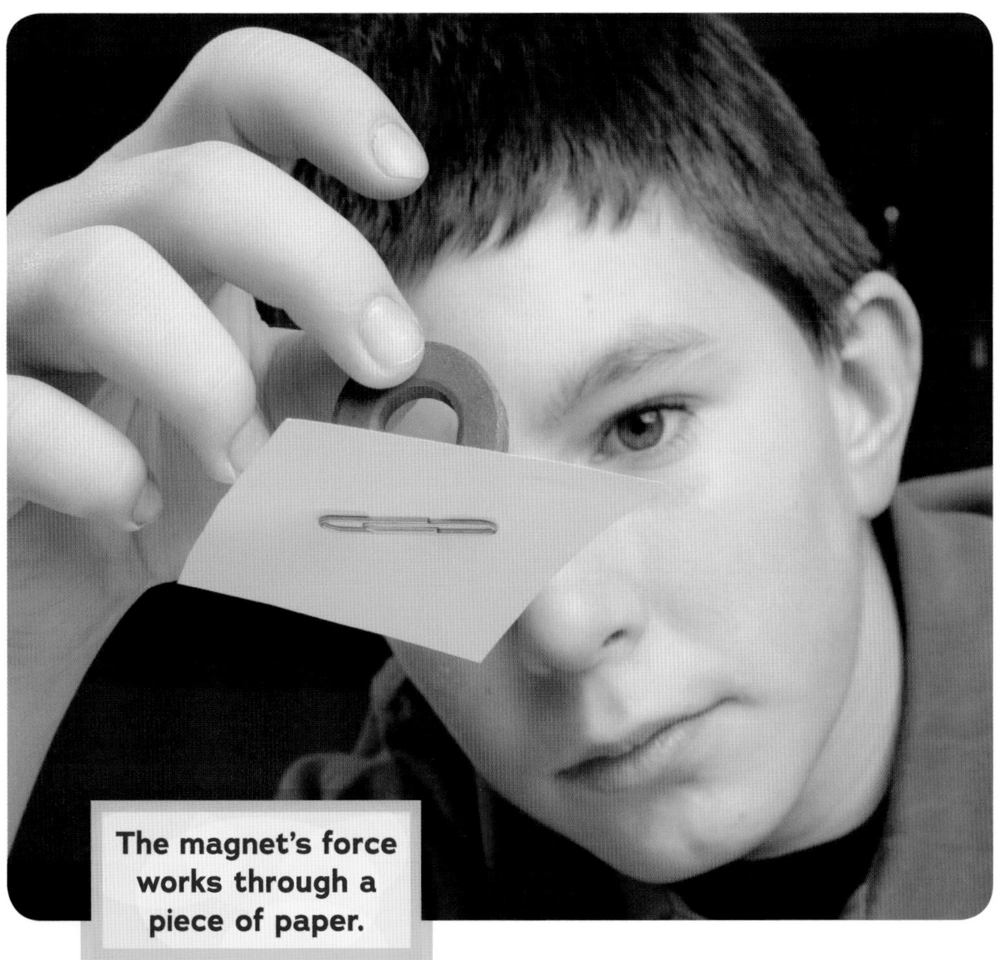

The magnet's force works through a piece of paper.

Magnetic force can act through your body too. Use your right hand to hold a magnet on top of your left pointer finger. Ask a friend to hold a paper clip under your finger, just below the magnet. Can your friend make the paper clip hang from your finger?

A strong magnet's force even works through your finger!

Chapter 5

KINDS OF MAGNETS

Some materials have many atoms with magnetic force. These atoms line up so their poles all point in the same direction. Because the magnetic atoms are lined up this way, the material has a lot of magnetic force.

All magnets are made of materials that have magnetic force. Why do these materials have magnetic force?

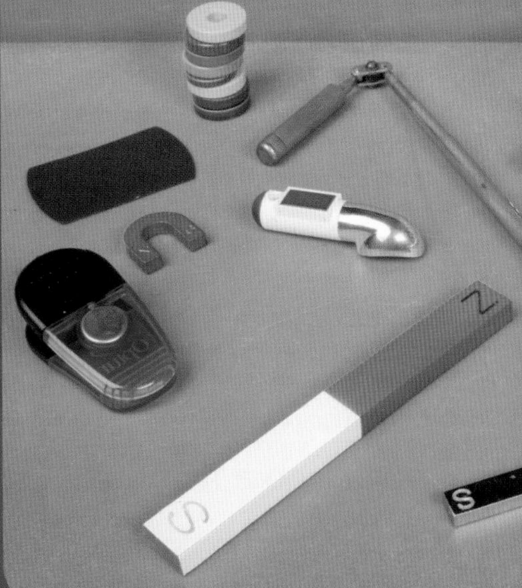

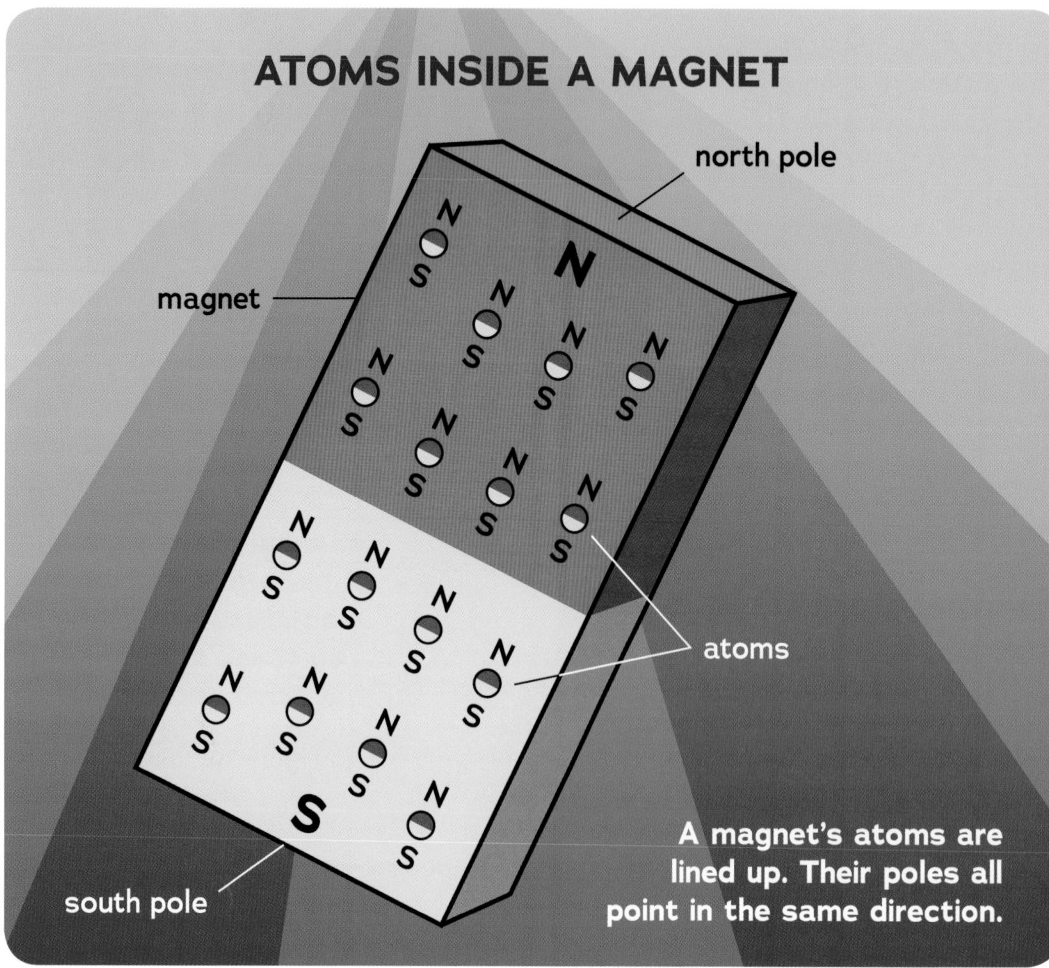

Iron and steel have many atoms with magnetic force. So objects made of iron and steel can become temporary magnets. You can prove this with two paper clips and a magnet.

Now Try This

Hold one paper clip near the other paper clip. Try to pick up the other clip with the first one. Are the paper clips attracted to each other? No. There is no magnetic force between them.

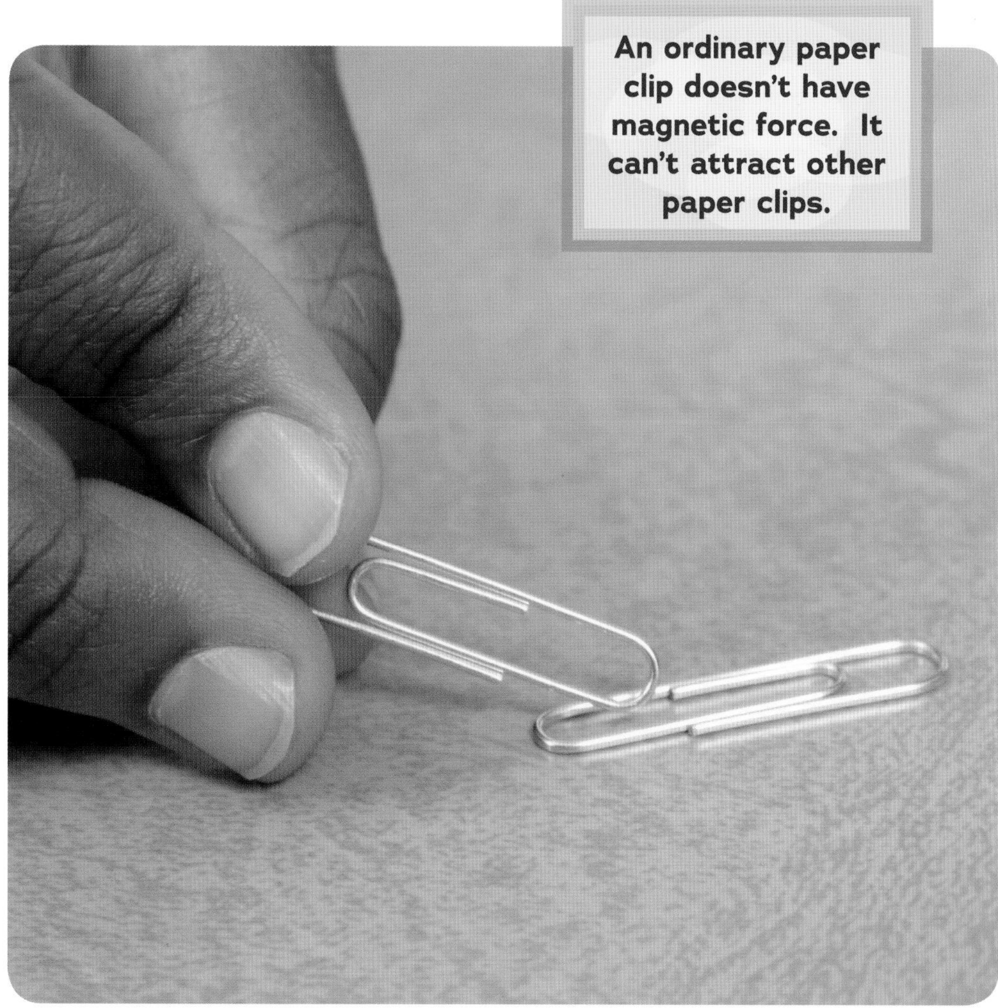

An ordinary paper clip doesn't have magnetic force. It can't attract other paper clips.

Put one paper clip on top of the magnet. Make sure one end of the clip sticks out. Hold the magnet so that the loose end of the clip is near the other paper clip. Is it attracted to the hanging paper clip? It is. Why does this happen?

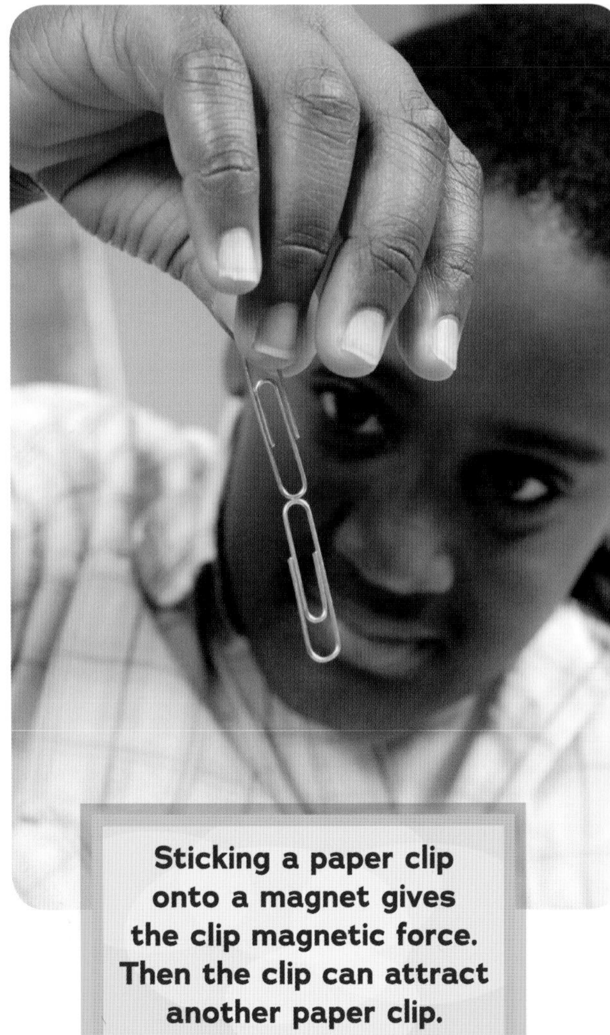

Sticking a paper clip onto a magnet gives the clip magnetic force. Then the clip can attract another paper clip.

A paper clip's atoms are like tiny magnets. The magnet's force makes the atoms line up so their poles point in the same direction. The paper clip becomes a temporary magnet.

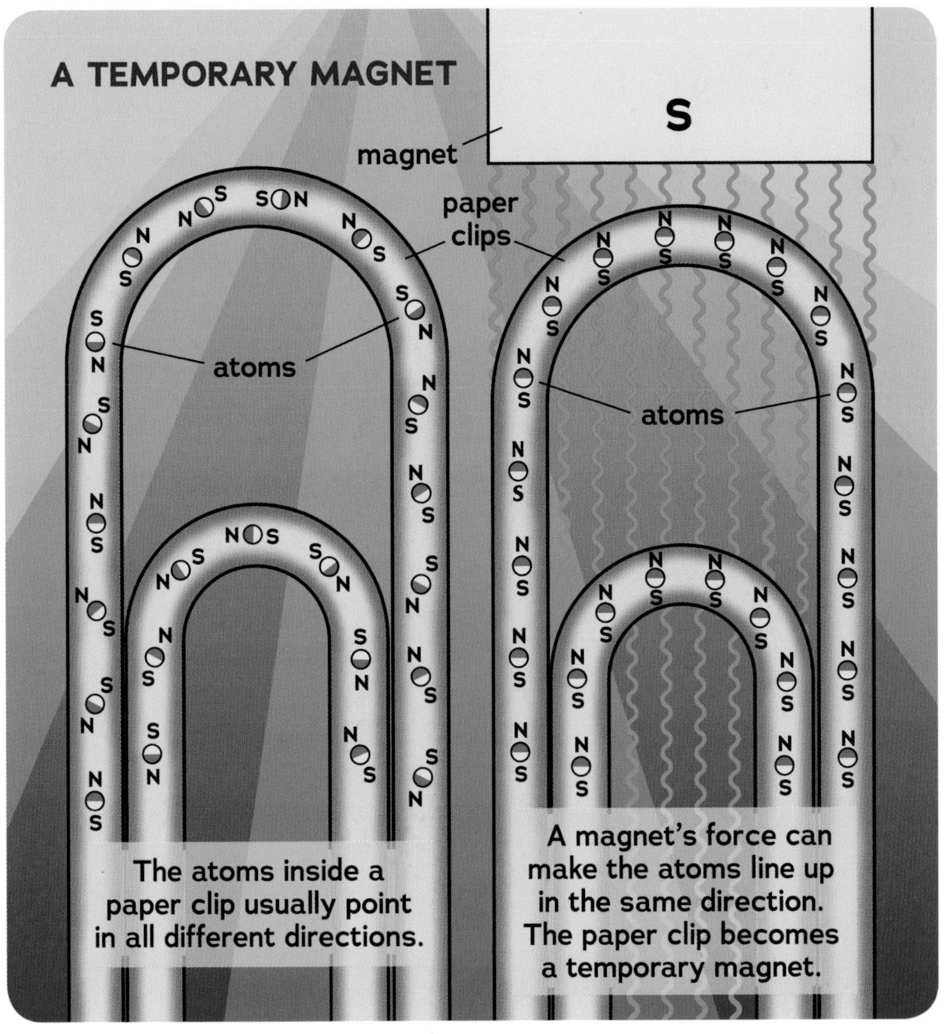

Sharply tap your paper clip magnet against a tabletop fifty times. Then hold it near the other paper clips. Does it attract them now? No. Tapping the paper clip knocked the atoms out of their neat lines. The magnetic force is gone.

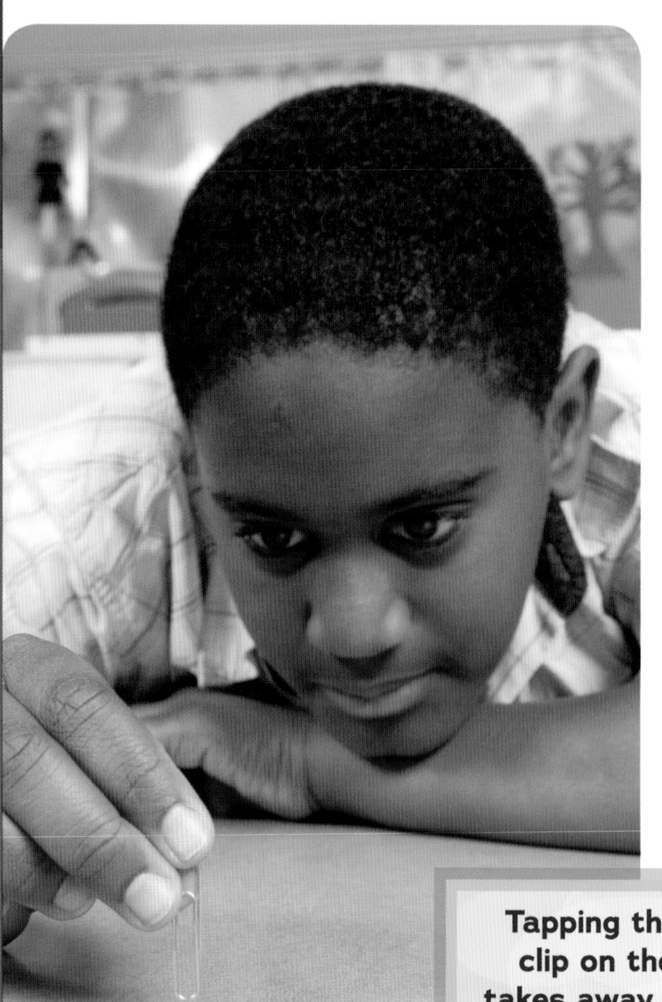

Tapping the paper clip on the table takes away the clip's magnetic force.

Electromagnets

Electricity can be used to make very strong temporary magnets. These magnets are called electromagnets. To make an electromagnet, wire is twisted into a coil. The wire can carry electricity. When electricity flows through the coil of wire, it makes a strong magnetic field. When the electricity is turned off, the magnetic force stops.

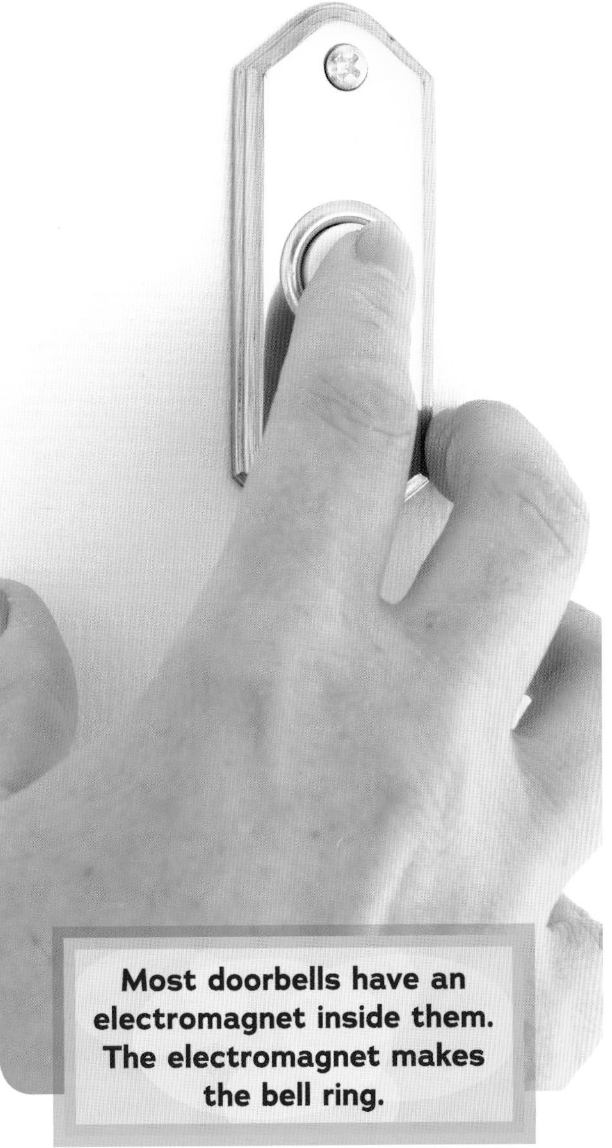

Most doorbells have an electromagnet inside them. The electromagnet makes the bell ring.

Earth: A Giant Electromagnet

The center of Earth is called the core. Earth's core is mostly made of iron. The core is very hot. So some of the iron in the core is melted. This melted iron is not a hard metal. Instead, it is a liquid. Electricity moves around in the liquid iron. The flowing electricity makes a magnetic field. Earth is a giant electromagnet!

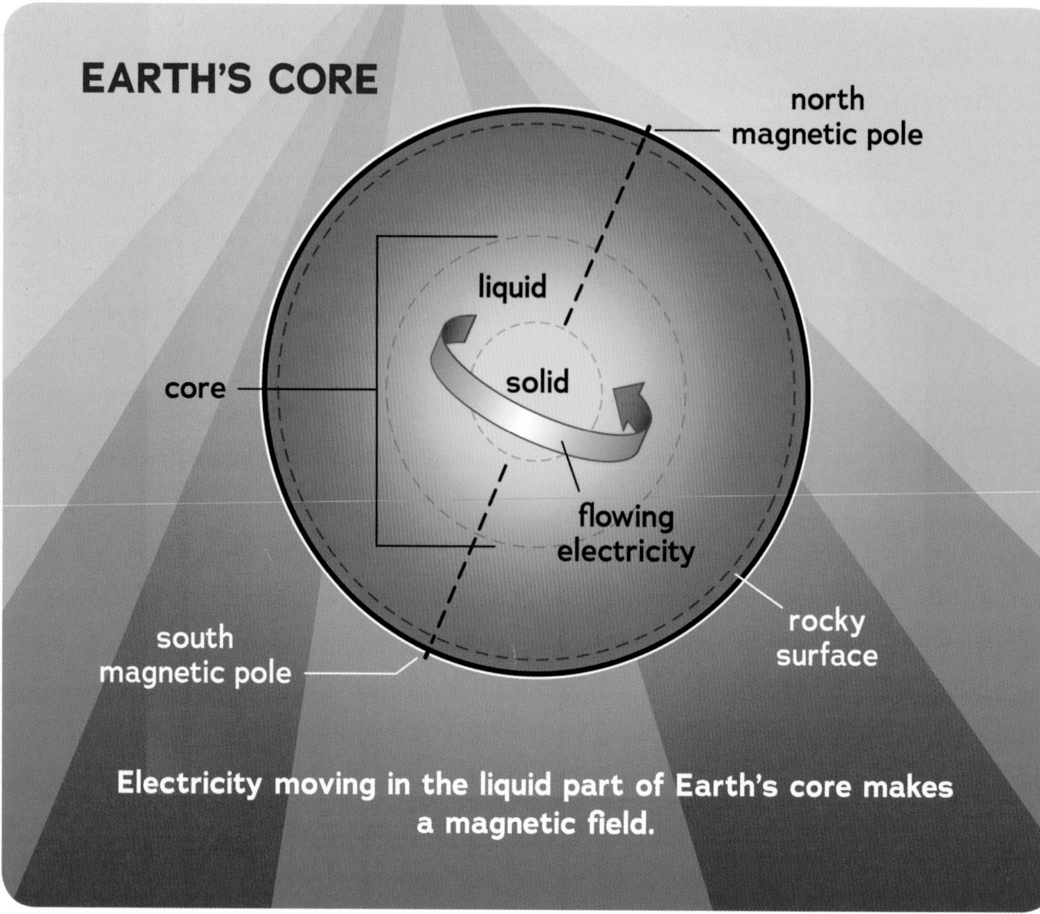

Electricity moving in the liquid part of Earth's core makes a magnetic field.

Some geese travel thousands of miles each year. The geese use Earth's magnetic field to find their way.

Some animals can sense Earth's magnetic field. Birds use Earth's magnetic field to find their way when they migrate. Migrating is traveling when the seasons change.

Magnetic force is an important part of our lives too. Magnets are inside most of the machines we use. Tiny magnets are inside computers. Large magnets lift heavy objects in junkyards. Magnets make our work easier. What magnets are working for you right now?

Glossary

atom: a very tiny particle that makes up all things

compass: a tool used to show direction. A compass's needle is a magnet that always points north.

electromagnet: a magnet that gets its magnetic force from electricity

electron: a tiny particle that circles around the center of an atom

force: a push or a pull

magnetic: a word to describe something that can be made into a magnet. Iron and steel are magnetic materials.

magnetic field: the space around a magnet where the magnet's force can attract an object

nonmagnetic: a word to describe something that cannot be made into a magnet. Paper and glass are nonmagnetic materials.

nucleus: the center of an atom

orbit: to travel in a circle

permanent: lasting forever

pole: the part of a magnet that has the strongest pulling power. Every magnet has a north pole and a south pole.

repel: to push away

temporary: lasting only for a short time

unlike: different

Learn More about Magnetism

Books

Meiani, Antonella. *Magnetism.* Minneapolis: Lerner Publications Company, 2003. This interesting title explains all about magnetism.

Taylor-Butler, Christine. *Super Cool Science Experiments: Magnets.* Ann Arbor, MI: Cherry Lake Publishing, 2010. Find more fun experiments in this book.

Vogel, Julia. *Push and Pull!: Learn about Magnets.* Mankato, MN: Child's World, 2010. Vogel provides a good basic introduction to magnets.

Woodford, Chris. *Experiments with Electricity and Magnetism.* New York: Gareth Stevens, 2010. This book includes experiments related to both magnetism and electricity.

Websites

BBC Bitesize Science: Magnets and Springs

http://www.bbc.co.uk/schools/ks2bitesize/science/physical_processes/magnet_springs/read1.shtml

This website is a good resource for students learning about magnets and magnetism.

Creative Kids at Home: Magnets

http://www.creativekidsathome.com/science/magnet.html

This site features trivia questions, activities, and more.

Energy Kids Page: Energy History

http://www.eia.doe.gov/kids/energy.cfm?page=4

Learn about the history of energy, including magnetism. This site also has information about some of the famous scientists who figured out how energy works.

Index

Photo Acknowledgments

Photographs copyright © Andy King. Additional images in this book are used with the permission of: © Bounce/UpperCut Images/Getty Images, p. 5; © Barbara Helgason/Dreamstime.com, p. 6; © Laura Westlund/Independent Picture Service, pp. 7, 20, 30, 33, 36; © Dan Van Den Broeke/Dreamstime.com, p. 10; © Stevies/Dreamstime.com, p. 35; © Gerry Lemmo, p. 37.

Front cover: © Steve Wisbauer/Stockbyte/Getty Images.

Main body text set in Adrianna Regular 14/20.
Typeface provided by Chank.